RAINFOREST

Om Books International

First Published in 2025 by

Om Books International

Corporate & Editorial Office
A-12, Sector 64, Noida 201 301
Uttar Pradesh, India
Phone: +91 120 477 4100
Email: editorial@ombooks.com
Website: www.ombooksinternational.com

Sales Office
107, Ansari Road, Darya Ganj
New Delhi 110 002, India
Phone: +91 11 4000 9000
Email: sales@ombooks.com
Website: www.ombooks.com

ISBN: 978-93-52761-73-9

Printed in India

10 9 8 7 6 5 4 3 2 1

CONTENTS

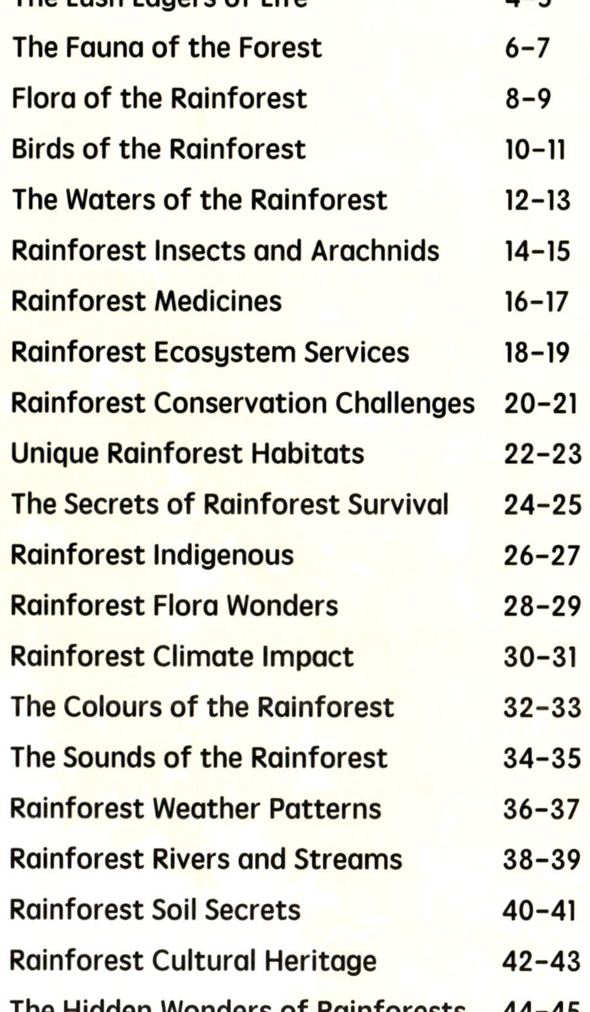

THE LUSH LAYERS OF LIFE

EMERGENT INSIGHT: TOWERS OF THE FOREST

The emergent layer features the tallest trees, standing up to 70 metres. These giants peek out above the canopy, providing nesting sites for eagles, butterflies, and bats. All these creatures rely on the high vantage points for survival and navigation.

Fun Fact

The Amazon Rainforest is the world's largest tropical rainforest. It is so vast that it spans across eight countries and covers approximately 5.5 million square km!

CANOPY CRUSADERS: THE DYNAMIC UPPER LAYER

The rainforest canopy, often over 30 metres above the ground, is a dense layer formed by the treetops. This dense layer blocks most sunlight, creating a unique world where 90% of rainforest organisms live. It is home to diverse birds, insects, and climbing mammals.

THE UNDERSTORY'S SECRET: LIFE IN THE SHADOWS

Below the canopy lies the understory, a low-light layer where plants must survive with as little as 5% of the sunlight. This area is teeming with snakes, jaguars, and leopards, which utilise the dense cover to ambush their prey.

VINES: THE RAINFOREST'S LIFELINES

Lianas, or woody vines, are integral to the rainforest structure, starting from the floor and climbing high into the canopy. They form structural pathways and provide support for many animals and plants. This allows different species to coexist. They also help with movement and provide access to the upper layers.

THE FOREST FLOOR: A DECOMPOSING WONDERLAND

The rainforest floor is dark and damp. It is covered in a thick layer of decomposing plant and animal matter. This layer is crucial as it provides nutrients to the forest. It is home to many decomposers, like fungi and termites, which break down organic matter to maintain the ecosystem's health.

THE FAUNA OF THE FOREST

JAGUARS:
THE STEALTHY PREDATORS OF THE UNDERBRUSH

Jaguars are the apex predators of the rainforest, adept at swimming and climbing. They primarily hunt on the forest floor but are known to venture into trees to catch unsuspecting prey from above.

HOWLER MONKEYS:
THE VOCAL LOCALS

Known for their loud howls, which can travel three miles through dense forests, howler monkeys are essential communicators in the rainforest. Their calls help to establish territory and warn others of threats, ensuring group safety.

Fun Fact

What makes a howler monkey so loud? A giant hyoid bone in its throat that turns every call into a rainforest-rattling roar!

POISON DART FROGS: DEADLY BEAUTIES

These vibrant frogs produce toxins strong enough to repel most predators. Indigenous tribes once used their poison on hunting darts, which is how they got their name. Despite their danger, they play a crucial role in the ecosystem by controlling insect populations.

SLOTH SECRETS: SLOW AND STEADY SURVIVORS

Sloths are renowned for their slow movement, an adaptation that helps conserve energy. Their fur hosts symbiotic algae which provides camouflage among the high branches.

HUMMINGBIRDS: THE NECTAR NAVIGATORS

Hummingbirds are crucial for pollination. They zip through the rainforest, visiting hundreds of flowers daily. Their high-speed wing flapping allows them to hover in place, making them the only birds capable of sustained backward flight.

FLORA OF THE RAINFOREST

Fun Fact

A single rainforest bromeliad can hold up to 10 litres of water in its leaf reservoirs!

THE RUBBER TREE: NATURE'S BOUNCY INNOVATION

Native to the Amazon, rubber trees were critical to the development of the rubber industry. The sap, or latex, from these trees is still used in many products from tyres to waterproof clothing.

ORCHIDS: JEWELS OF THE CANOPY

Rainforests are home to over 20,000 orchid species, which decorate the canopy with their vivid blooms. Their intricate relationship with pollinators, like bees and moths, exemplifies coevolution.

CACAO'S SWEET BEGINNINGS: THE CHOCOLATE SEED

Cacao trees are found in the understory. They bear pods which are the raw ingredient of chocolate. This cherished treat has ancient ceremonial uses dating back to the Maya and Aztec civilisations.

GIANT WATER LILIES: SURFACE SENTINELS

The giant water lily supports up to 40 kg. Its leaves have a special structure with air pockets. These air pockets help the leaves float on the water's surface. These plants are not only a habitat for fish, but also act as natural water purifiers.

BROMELIADS: RAINWATER COLLECTORS

Bromeliads have adapted to collect rainwater in their central cups. These cups create small habitats for various creatures. Frog tadpoles, mosquito larvae, and other fauna rely on them. This shows the interdependence within rainforest ecosystems.

BIRDS OF THE RAINFOREST

HARPY EAGLES: THE AERIAL HUNTERS

The harpy eagle, one of the largest and most powerful eagles, thrives in the rainforest canopy. They are adept hunters. Due to their formidable talons and keen vision they are capable of snatching monkeys and sloths right from the trees.

Fun Fact

The call of the Screaming Piha is considered one of the loudest in the animal kingdom. It is a common sound in the Amazon rainforest.

TOUCANS: THE ICONIC BEAKS

Recognisable by their large, colourful bills, toucans are not just a tropical icon but vital for forest regeneration. They eat a wide variety of fruits. They also help in dispersing the seeds throughout the forest, aiding in plant propagation.

SCARLET MACAWS: THE VIVID VOCALISTS

These striking birds have bright red, yellow, and blue feathers. They are more than just visually stunning. Their loud calls and social behaviour help keep their flocks together. This strengthens their chances of survival in the dense jungle.

KING VULTURE: THE SCAVENGER SOVEREIGN

King vultures have a distinctive look with their white and black bodies and a colourful head. They play a crucial role in the ecosystem by consuming dead animals. This prevents the spread of disease within the forest.

COCK-OF-THE-ROCK: THE FLAMBOYANT PERFORMER

The male Andean cock-of-the-rock performs elaborate mating dances. These displays are not only a treat for birdwatchers but also critical for the species' breeding success. They are also known for their vivid orange plumage and fan-shaped crest.

THE WATERS OF THE RAINFOREST

Fun Fact

Water lilies in the Amazon can grow so large that their leaves can hold a small child.

AMAZON RIVER DOLPHIN: THE PINK NAVIGATOR

The Amazon river dolphin, or boto, is known for its striking pink colouration and flexible neck. These features allow it to navigate the flooded forests during the wet season, searching for fish and crustaceans.

PIRANHAS: THE FEARSOME FISH

Despite their fearsome reputation, piranhas are primarily scavengers. The sound of splashing can trigger a feeding frenzy. While dangerous, this helps clean up excess organic matter in rivers.

ELECTRIC EELS: THE SHOCKING PREDATORS

Electric eels can generate an electric shock of up to 600 volts to stun prey or defend themselves. This remarkable adaptation makes them one of the most formidable predators in freshwater habitats.

ARAPAIMA: THE GIANT OF THE AMAZON

The arapaima is one of the world's largest freshwater fish. It can grow over 3 meters long and weigh up to 200 kilograms. Their ability to breathe air allows them to inhabit oxygen-poor waters where other fish would perish.

CAIMANS: THE RAINFOREST'S REPTILES

Caimans are essential for maintaining the ecological balance of rainforest waterways. They help control fish populations and are a key species for the health of aquatic ecosystems.

RAINFOREST INSECTS AND ARACHNIDS

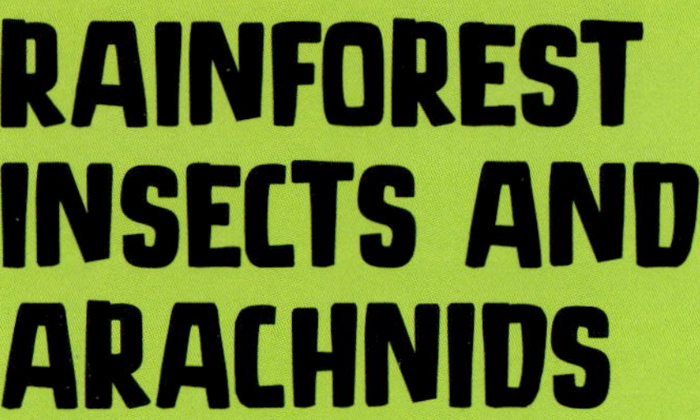

Fun Fact

Some rainforest frogs can resist the poisons of the insects they eat. This immunity protects them from harm. They use their predators' weapons as their own defense.

LEAFCUTTER ANTS: THE ULTIMATE FARMERS

These industrious insects cut leaves to cultivate fungus, their primary food source. This unique form of agriculture is highly efficient. It sustains vast colonies with millions of creatures.

TARANTULAS: THE GENTLE GIANTS

Despite their fearsome appearance, rainforest tarantulas are mostly harmless to humans. They help control insect populations and serve as prey for larger animals. This makes them an important part of the food web.

BUTTERFLIES: THE COLOURFUL MIGRANTS

Rainforests are home to thousands of butterfly species, many of which undertake significant migrations. These journeys help pollinate distant plants, ensuring genetic diversity and forest health.

WALKING STICKS: THE MASTERS OF DISGUISE

These insects blend seamlessly into their surroundings. They mimic twigs and branches to avoid predators. Their camouflage is a fascinating example of evolutionary adaptation for survival.

GOLIATH BEETLES: AMONG THE HEAVIEST INSECTS

Named after the biblical giant, Goliath beetles can weigh up to 100 grams in their larval stage. They are not only among the largest of all insects but also crucial decomposers in the rainforest ecosystem.

RAINFOREST MEDICINES

QUININE: NATURE'S FEVER FIGHTER

Extracted from the bark of the cinchona tree, quinine was the first effective treatment for malaria. This discovery in the 1600s revolutionised medicine and remains a critical component in the fight against this deadly disease.

Fun Fact

Over 25% of Western pharmaceuticals come from rainforest ingredients. However, less than 1% of tropical trees and plants have been tested for medicinal properties.

CURARE: FROM POISON TO PRESCRIPTION

Indigenous tribes traditionally used curare as a paralysing poison on blowgun darts. Today, it is used in modern medicine to relax muscles during surgery. This highlights the rainforest's contribution to medical science.

CAMU CAMU: THE VITAMIN C POWERHOUSE

This small, sour berry is native to the Amazon rainforest. It boasts the highest natural vitamin C content of any plant on earth. It's a vital ingredient in nutritional supplements for boosting immune health.

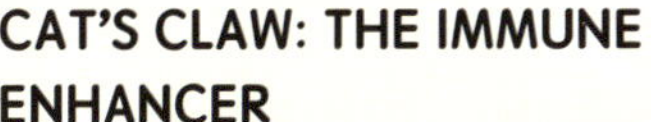

CAT'S CLAW: THE IMMUNE ENHANCER

Locally known as 'Una de Gato', cat's claw is a vine with powerful anti-inflammatory properties. It has been used to treat various health issues, including arthritis, digestive problems, and viral infections.

ACAI BERRIES: THE ANTIOXIDANT ANTHEMS

Acai berries are rich in antioxidants, which help combat ageing and boost brain function. They have become a popular superfood around the world, originating from the Amazon rainforest.

RAINFOREST ECOSYSTEM SERVICES

CARBON STORAGE: THE GREEN LUNGS

Tropical rainforests absorb large amounts of CO_2, helping to reduce climate change. Their ability to store carbon is crucial in the fight against global warming. This highlights the importance of protecting these ecosystems.

Fun Fact

A single rainforest tree can release about 760 litres of water into the atmosphere each year. This is equal to the amount of water used in nearly four showers!

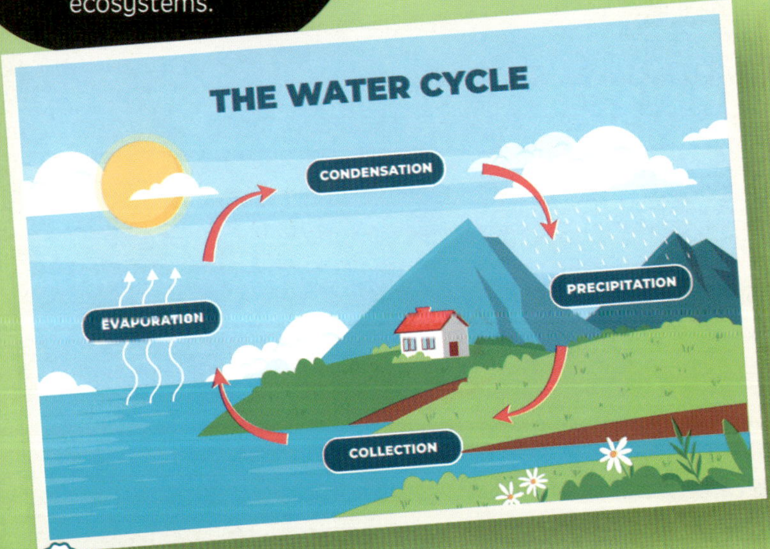

THE WATER CYCLE

CONDENSATION

PRECIPITATION

EVAPORATION

COLLECTION

WATER CYCLE REGULATION: THE ATMOSPHERIC RIVERS

Rainforests help maintain the global water cycle by releasing water vapour into the atmosphere. Then, it condenses and falls as rain around the world, supporting agriculture and drinking supplies.

SOIL EROSION PREVENTION: THE GROUND PROTECTORS

The vast root systems of rainforest trees help stabilise the soil, preventing erosion. This keeps the land fertile for agriculture and supports the health of the forest.

BIODIVERSITY HAVENS: THE GENETIC LIBRARIES

Rainforests are the most biodiverse habitats on Earth. They house millions of species, many of which are yet to be documented. This biodiversity is not only a treasure trove of discovery, but also crucial for ecological stability.

POLLINATION AND SEED DISPERSAL: NATURE'S GARDENERS

The rainforest is teeming with creatures that pollinate plants. They disperse seeds, ensuring forest regeneration and resilience. These natural processes are essential for the survival of countless species, including many crops vital to human agriculture.

RAINFOREST CONSERVATION CHALLENGES

DEFORESTATION: THE VANISHING VEIL

Deforestation due to logging, agriculture, and mining is the most significant threat to rainforests. It is stripping the Earth of its vital organs at an alarming rate and leading to habitat loss and species extinction.

Fun Fact

Rainforests are home to more than half of the Earth's plant and animal species. Amazingly, they cover only 6% of the world's land surface!

CLIMATE CHANGE: THE HEAT IS ON

Global warming alters rainfall patterns. It affects the rainforest health and leads to issues like drought and forest fires, which threaten these vital ecosystems.

ILLEGAL WILDLIFE TRADE: THE SILENT SMUGGLERS

The illegal trade in exotic wildlife for pets, medicine, and souvenirs puts numerous species at risk. It disrupts the ecological balance necessary for the forest's survival.

INVASIVE SPECIES: THE UNINVITED GUESTS

Non-native species introduced intentionally or accidentally outcompete local flora and fauna. They lead to a loss of biodiversity and alter rainforest ecology.

POLLUTION: THE TOXIC TAINT

Pollution from nearby urban, industrial, and agricultural activities can contaminate rainforest waterways and soil. This can harm both plant and animal life.

UNIQUE RAINFOREST HABITATS

MANGROVES: THE COASTAL GUARDIANS

Mangrove forests are found along coastlines where saltwater and freshwater mix. They provide critical nursery habitats for fish and crustaceans. Their tangled root systems not only support a diverse range of life but also protect shorelines from erosion and storm surges.

CLOUD FORESTS: THE MISTY REALMS

Higher in elevation than typical rainforests, cloud forests are often shrouded in persistent mist or cloud cover. This unique environment supports species that rely on constant moisture, such as mosses, orchids, and bromeliads.

Fun Fact

Bamboo can grow up to 91 cm in a single day, making it one of the fastest-growing plants on Earth!

PEAT SWAMPS: CARBON STORING POWERHOUSES

Peat swamp forests are waterlogged ecosystems filled with decomposing plant material. They are incredibly efficient at storing carbon, which helps combat climate change. However, during droughts, they become highly vulnerable to fires.

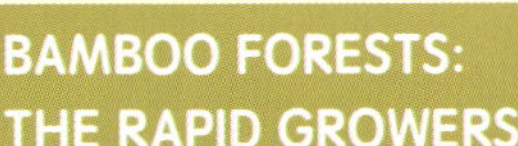

FLOODED RAINFORESTS: THE SEASONAL AQUATICS

Seasonally flooded forests, such as the várzea in the Amazon, undergo periods of flooding. The trees can be submerged for half the year! This dynamic environment supports species adapted to both aquatic and terrestrial life.

BAMBOO FORESTS: THE RAPID GROWERS

Bamboo forests are found within larger rainforests. They are characterised by the fast-growing bamboo that dominates these areas. These forests are crucial for certain wildlife, including the bamboo lemur and various bird species that depend on bamboo.

THE SECRETS OF RAINFOREST SURVIVAL

CAMOUFLAGE: THE ART OF HIDING

Many rainforest species have developed remarkable camouflage to blend into their surroundings. For example, the leaf-tailed gecko mimics the appearance of a leaf to avoid predators.

MUTUALISM: LIVING TOGETHER

Rainforests are full of examples of mutualism, where two species benefit from their relationship. For instance, the acacia tree and certain ant species live in mutual support. The tree provides shelter and food for the ants, which in return protect the tree from herbivores.

Fun Fact

The Amazon Rainforest produces about 20% of the world's oxygen, earning it the nickname 'the lungs of the Earth.'

NOCTURNAL LIFESTYLES: THE NIGHT SHIFT

Many rainforest animals are nocturnal to escape the daytime heat and reduce competition for resources. Creatures like the kinkajou use the cover of darkness to hunt and forage, conserving energy and avoiding predators.

EPIPHYTES: LIVING ON AIR

Plants like orchids, ferns, and bromeliads are epiphytes, growing on other plants instead of the soil. This adaptation allows them to reach the light and moisture available in the upper layers of the forest.

POISON AS PROTECTION: NATURE'S CHEMICAL WEAPONS

Numerous rainforest species, such as poison dart frogs, use toxins as a defense mechanism. These toxins help deter predators. They give species a crucial survival advantage in the competitive rainforest.

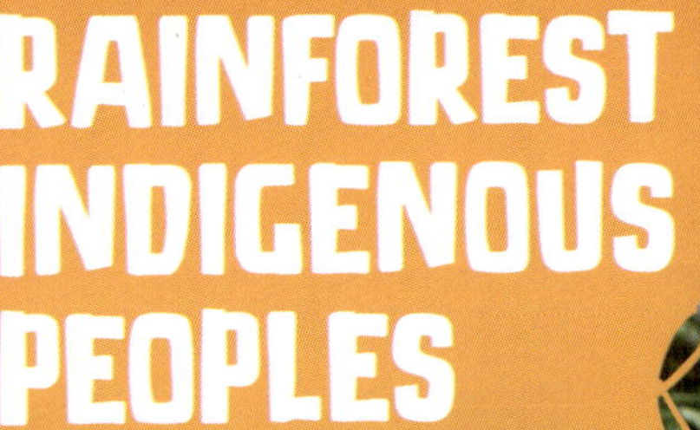

RAINFOREST INDIGENOUS PEOPLES

SUSTAINABLE PRACTICES: THE ECO PROTECTORS

Many Indigenous practices include sustainable farming, hunting, and forest management methods that minimise environmental impact. Examples include shifting cultivation and natural pest control.

KNOWLEDGE KEEPERS: THE TRIBAL WISDOM

Indigenous tribes have lived in harmony with the rainforest for thousands of years. They hold invaluable knowledge about its plants and animals. This traditional wisdom is crucial for both ecological research and conservation efforts.

Fun Fact

There are over 400 distinct indigenous groups in the Amazon Rainforest alone, speaking roughly 300 different languages!

SPIRITUAL CONNECTIONS: THE FOREST AS SACRED

Rainforests hold deep spiritual significance for indigenous peoples. They are often seen as sacred places that are central to their cultural identity and heritage.

GUARDIANS OF BIODIVERSITY: THE CONSERVATION LEADERS

Indigenous communities play a key role in protecting rainforest habitats. They actively oppose deforestation and illegal mining, which threaten both their homes and the forest's biodiversity.

CULTURAL DIVERSITY: THE HUMAN MOSAIC

The rainforest is home to a remarkable variety of Indigenous cultures. Each has its own language, traditions, and unique connection to the environment. This cultural richness adds another layer of value to these ecosystems.

RAINFOREST FLORA WONDERS

GIANT KAPOK TREE: THE FOREST'S SKYSCRAPER

The Kapok tree, or Ceiba tree, towers above the rainforest canopy, reaching heights of over 70 meters. It serves as an important ecological hub, providing habitat and food for numerous rainforest species.

Fun Fact

The Rafflesia flower can grow up to 1 metre in diameter and weigh up to 10 kilograms!

STRANGLER FIG: THE LETHAL EMBRACE

The strangler fig begins its life as a seed in the canopy, sending roots down and around a host tree. Over time, it envelops and eventually kills the tree. This aggressive growth strategy helps the fig thrive in the competitive upper canopy.

MEDICINAL MARVELS: THE PHARMACY TREE

Many rainforest trees, like the cinchona and rubber trees, have been traditional sources of medicine for centuries. These 'pharmacy trees' continue to be vital in modern medicine for their healing compounds.

CARNIVOROUS PITCHER PLANTS: THE INSECT TRAPS

Pitcher plants thrive in nutrient-poor soils by luring, trapping, and digesting insects. This remarkable adaptation helps them supplement their nutritional intake and survive in challenging environments.

RAFFLESIA: THE WORLD'S LARGEST BLOOM

The Rafflesia, known for producing the largest single flower on Earth, is a parasitic plant. It emits a strong odour of decaying flesh to attract insects for pollination.

RAINFOREST CLIMATE IMPACT

HEAT REGULATION: THE GLOBAL THERMOSTAT

Rainforests absorb vast quantities of heat from the sun. They play a crucial role in regulating global temperatures and climate patterns.

Fun Fact

A single tree in the Amazon can store up to 160 kilograms of carbon annually. This is equivalent to the emissions of driving a car for over 1,000 kilometres!

MOISTURE RESERVOIR: THE HUMIDITY HAVEN

The dense vegetation of rainforests releases enormous amounts of water vapour into the atmosphere. This significantly contributes to global precipitation and humidity levels.

WIND PATTERNS: NATURE'S WEATHER SYSTEMS

Rainforests influence local and global wind patterns through evapotranspiration. This process affects weather systems far beyond their geographical boundaries.

CARBON SINK: THE CLIMATE STABILIZER

Rainforests act as major carbon sinks, absorbing and storing carbon dioxide. This helps offset greenhouse gas emissions and fight climate change.

OZONE LAYER PROTECTION: THE UV SHIELD

Rainforests release compounds that interact with the atmosphere, helping to maintain the ozone layer. This protective layer shields life on Earth from harmful ultraviolet rays.

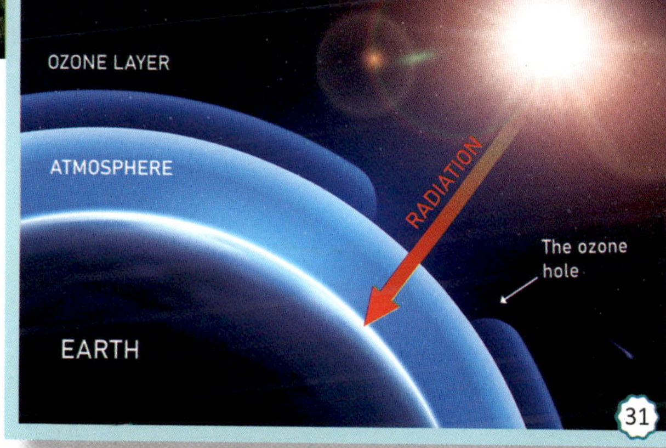

THE COLOURS OF THE RAINFOREST

Fun Fact

The iridescent scales on a butterfly's wings can deflect bacteria and dirt, keeping them clean and free from infections.

FLAMBOYANT FLOWERS: THE SPECTRUM SPLENDOUR

Rainforest flowers display a stunning range of colours to attract diverse pollinators. Birds, bats, and insects are each drawn to specific hues and scents.

BRIGHT BIRDS: THE FEATHERED RAINBOWS

Birds like the scarlet macaw and blue-and-gold macaw have vibrant plumage that helps them in multiple ways. Their bright colours attract mates while also providing camouflage among the colourful rainforest flowers and fruits.

COLOURFUL FROGS: THE VIVID WARNING

The bright colours of poison dart frogs warn predators of their toxicity. This survival strategy is called aposematism.

FRUITFUL DISPLAYS: THE EDIBLE ATTRACTIONS

The diverse fruits of the rainforest, like mangoes, bananas, and papayas, play a crucial role in attracting animals. These animals eat the fruit and help disperse the seeds, aiding in forest regeneration.

BUTTERFLY WINGS: THE FLOATING ART

The wings of rainforest butterflies, such as the Blue Morpho, are masterpieces of nature. Their iridescent colours are not pigments but are created by the structure of their wings reflecting light.

THE SOUNDS OF THE RAINFOREST

FROG SYMPHONIES: THE NIGHTTIME CONCERT

At night, the rainforest comes alive with the calls of frogs and toads. Each species has a unique call that helps attract mates and ward off rivals. Together, these sounds create a complex chorus that echoes through the trees.

POTOOS: THE GHOSTLY NOCTURNALS

Potoos are nocturnal birds famous for their eerie, haunting calls that sound almost supernatural. They use these vocalisations to communicate in the pitch-black night. Their calls add to the mysterious soundscape of the rainforest after dark.

Fun Fact

The pitch of a cicada's song is so high that it can be on the edge of human hearing. It is used to deter predators by confusing their sonar systems.

BIRDSONG MELODIES: THE AVIAN ORCHESTRA

The rainforest's diverse birdlife fills the air with a symphony of sounds. From the melodious whistles of songbirds to the harsh squawks of parrots, each species adds to the vibrant chorus. These sounds play a crucial role in mating rituals and territorial disputes.

INSECT BUZZES: THE CONSTANT HUM

Insects like cicadas and beetles create a constant buzz, forming the signature soundtrack of the rainforest. These sounds are not only communication tools, but also serve to confuse predators.

THE RUSTLE OF LEAVES: NATURE'S WHISPER

The rustling of leaves in the wind, along with the occasional crash of a falling branch or fruit, reflects the rainforest's constant cycle of life and death. Every sound tells a story of survival.

RAINFOREST WEATHER PATTERNS

TORRENTIAL RAINS: THE LIFELINE OF THE FOREST

Rainforests receive over 2000 mm of rain annually, a key factor in their lush biodiversity. These frequent, heavy rains are vital for sustaining the ecosystem's health and vitality.

Fun Fact

Rainforest plants are so effective at recycling water that 75% of the rain falling on the forest is returned to the atmosphere through evapotranspiration.

MISTY MORNINGS: THE FOGGY VEIL

Early morning fog is a common sight in rainforests, delivering essential moisture to plants and animals. It is especially important for the understory and forest floor, which receive little direct sunlight.

SUNLIGHT SHAFTS: THE RARE GLIMPSES

Gaps in the canopy let shafts of sunlight reach the forest floor, creating vital hotspots. These areas support the growth of certain plants and provide warmth for cold-blooded animals.

VARIABLE TEMPERATURES: THE THERMAL LAYERS

Rainforest temperatures vary between the ground and the canopy. The canopy is often several degrees warmer due to direct sunlight and trapped rising heat from the forest floor.

HIGH HUMIDITY: THE SATURATED AIR

Rainforests maintain consistently high humidity, fostering the growth of fungi and bacteria. This aids in decomposition, recycling nutrients back into the soil.

RAINFOREST RIVERS AND STREAMS

Fun Fact

Piranhas, often feared, play an essential role in the ecosystem by scavenging dead and decaying matter. This helps keep river habitats clean and nutrient-rich.

WATERFALLS: THE CASCADING BEAUTIES

Many rainforest rivers feature stunning waterfalls, creating breathtaking landscapes. These waterfalls also help oxygenate the water, supporting diverse aquatic habitats.

CLEARWATER RIVERS: THE CRYSTAL FLOW

Clearwater rivers, unlike their sediment-rich brownwater counterparts, have low nutrient levels. However, they support unique ecosystems with species specially adapted to these conditions.

BLACKWATER RIVERS: THE DARK WATERS

The dark colour of blackwater rivers comes from tannins released by decomposing plant matter. While less hospitable to mosquitoes, these rivers support specialised fish species.

FLOOD PULSE: THE SEASONAL LIFELINE

Many rainforest rivers experience an annual flood pulse, temporarily expanding their banks. This process delivers essential nutrients to floodplain forests, helping sustain biodiversity.

RIPARIAN ZONES: THE VITAL MARGINS

Riparian zones, the areas along riverbanks, play a crucial role in maintaining water quality. They also provide vital habitats for wildlife and serve as natural buffers between water and land.

RAINFOREST SOIL SECRETS

MYCORRHIZAL FUNGI: THE HIDDEN NETWORK

These fungi form symbiotic relationships with plant roots, extending deep into the soil. They help plants absorb more nutrients and water, enhancing their growth and survival. This underground network is vital for the health of rainforest ecosystems.

Fun Fact

A single tablespoon of rainforest soil can hold billions of bacteria and fungi. These microorganisms, representing hundreds of species, play a vital role in nutrient cycling within the ecosystem.

NUTRIENT CYCLING: THE RAPID RECYCLERS

Despite their lush appearance, rainforest soils are often nutrient-poor because nutrients are rapidly recycled. Warm, humid conditions accelerate decomposition, returning nutrients to the environment almost immediately.

TERRA PRETA: THE ANCIENT SUPER SOIL

Found in the Amazon, terra preta is a fertile soil created by Indigenous people by adding charcoal, bone, and organic waste. Unlike most rainforest soils, it has remained nutrient-rich for centuries.

LEAF LITTER LAYER: THE FOREST'S BLANKET

The rainforest floor is covered with fallen leaves, branches, and dead plants. This layer protects the soil from erosion and provides habitat for countless organisms that enrich soil health.

SOIL EROSION: THE CONSTANT THREAT

Where rainforests have been cleared, soil erosion can become a severe problem. Without tree roots to anchor the soil and the canopy to shield it from heavy rains, valuable topsoil washes away. This erosion reduces the land's fertility and disrupts the ecosystem.

RAINFOREST CULTURAL HERITAGE

INDIGENOUS ART: EXPRESSIONS OF THE FOREST

Art forms like painting, weaving, and carving are central to rainforest cultures, often drawing from the forest's materials and rich biodiversity. These practices are not just artistic but also carry deep cultural and spiritual meaning.

Fun Fact

The Boa people of the Amazon have a tradition where they believe trees are ancestral spirits. They perform ceremonies to communicate with these spirits for guidance and blessings.

SHAMANIC TRADITIONS: THE SPIRITUAL HEALERS

Shamans are vital to many rainforest communities, drawing on ancestral knowledge to heal with natural remedies. They also protect their people through spiritual practices.

FOLKLORE AND MYTHS: THE STORYTELLING LEGACY

Rainforest tribes have a rich tradition of storytelling. They use myths and legends to explain natural phenomena and teach important life lessons. These stories are an integral part of community identity and cohesion.

CEREMONIAL RITUALS: THE RHYTHMS OF LIFE

Many rainforest societies hold rituals and ceremonies to mark important life events and seasonal changes. These traditions often include music, dance, and traditional costumes, reflecting their deep connection to the environment.

SUSTAINABLE LIVING: THE ECO-CENTRIC LIFESTYLE

Traditional rainforest dwellers have developed sustainable lifestyles, using techniques that let them live off the land without depleting it. Their way of life serves as a model of conservation and harmony with nature.

THE HIDDEN WONDERS OF RAINFORESTS

EARLY HUMAN HABITATION

Archaeological evidence suggests that humans inhabited the rainforests of West Africa 150,000 years ago, much earlier than previously believed. This discovery reshapes our understanding of human migration and adaptation.

NEW SPECIES DISCOVERY: THE LEGLESS AMPHIBIAN

A new species of legless amphibian, the truncated caecilian (Caecilia truncata), was recently found in the Ecuadorian rainforest. This pale grey, 19-inch creature resembles an earthworm but has rows of needle-like teeth.

AMAZON FIRES SURGE

In 2024, fires in the Brazilian Amazon destroyed 44.2 million acres, a staggering 66% increase from the previous year. Climate change, illegal logging, and deforestation contribute to this crisis, threatening biodiversity.

BIODIVERSITY HOTSPOTS IN DECLINE

Only about 25% of the world's remaining tropical rainforests are in good condition. The rest are either degraded or at risk, making conservation efforts more critical than ever.

MINING-INDUCED DEFORESTATION

Mining activities for metals, minerals, and coal have caused nearly 1.4 million hectares of tropical forest loss between 2001 and 2020. The biggest deforestation hotspots include Indonesia and Brazil.

TECHNOLOGICAL ADVANCEMENTS AND CONSERVATION CHALLENGES

LIDAR TECHNOLOGY REVEALS AMAZON'S SECRETS

The Amazônia Revelada project uses advanced Lidar technology to map hidden archaeological structures in the Amazon rainforest. This includes 30 previously unknown sites, such as ancient settlements and an eighteenth-century Portuguese village.

SPECIES DISCOVERIES AMID CONFLICT IN COLOMBIA

Scientists gained access to previously unreachable rainforest regions in Colombia following the 2016 peace deal, leading to numerous species discoveries. However, renewed violence now endangers both researchers and wildlife.

STAR TREK FROGS: NEW SPECIES WITH UNIQUE CALLS

In Madagascar, 7 new tree frog species have been discovered, each making high-pitched calls reminiscent of 'Star Trek' sound effects. Some have even been named after famous Star Trek captains.

CELTIC RAINFOREST IN WALES AT RISK

The ancient temperate rainforests of Wales are home to unique biodiversity. They are in decline, with only 20% of surveyed sites in good condition. Conservationists are urging action to protect these rare forests.

SEEDLING INSIGHTS FOR RAINFOREST RESTORATION

New research shows that seedlings from wet rainforest sites grow just as well under drought conditions as those from dry sites. This simplifies seed sourcing for reforestation projects, enhancing rainforest restoration efforts.

Titles in this Series

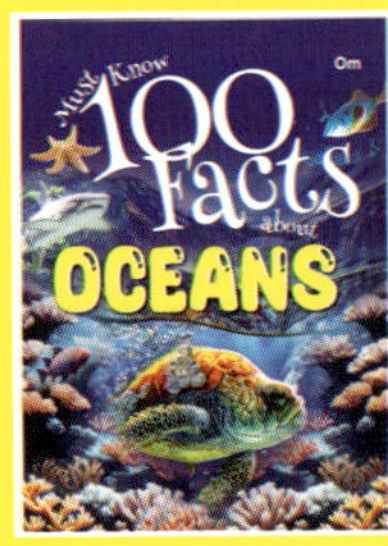

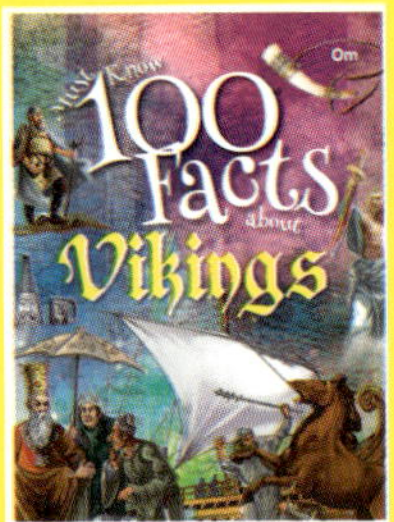

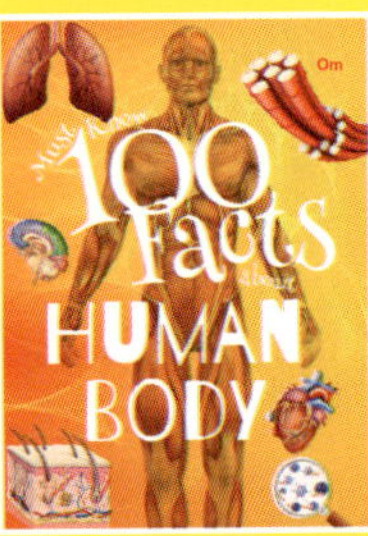

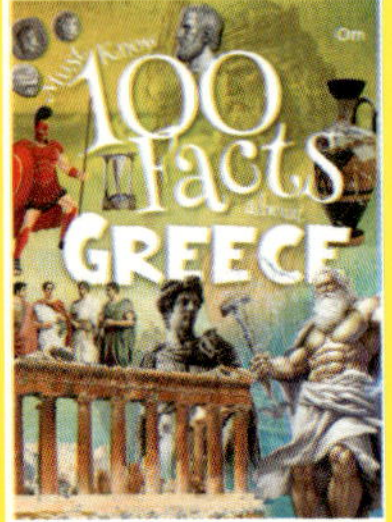

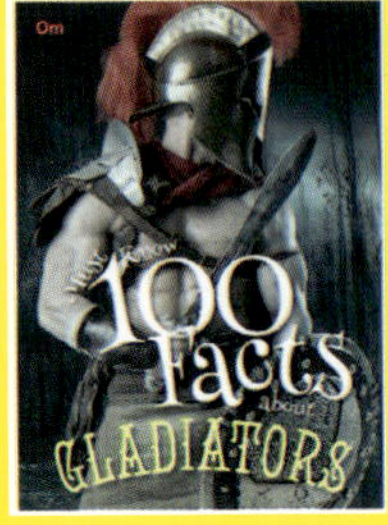

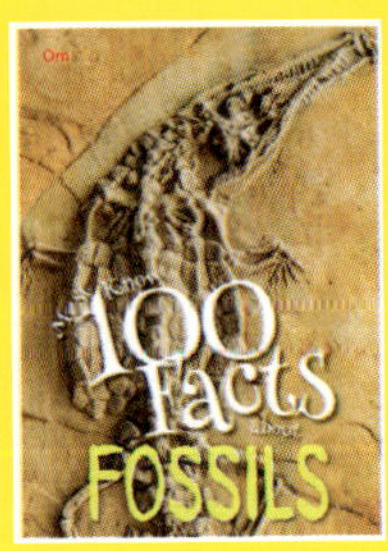

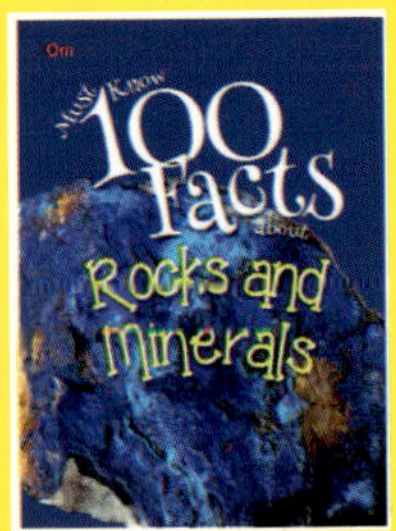